There was once an old grandmother with many, many grandchildren. She liked to make presents for them and had decided to make each of them a teddy bear. For days and days she sat at her sewing machine and sewed.

Finally, late one night, all of the teddy bears were ready. The grandmother, tired from all her hard work, fell asleep at her sewing machine. Suddenly, as if by magic, the little bears began to whisper to each other.

One bear thought it would be fun to have even more friends. He found a drawing board and began to draw.

TOMMY

TIMMY

SCOTTIE

BANDIT

DUNK

JUMBO

VIOLET

THE CAPTAIN

TEDDY

WALLY

DR. SPOTTY

PC STOP

MR. PIGGLES

PIGLET

MRS. PIGGLES

VON FOX

MOLE

TIGER

RUSTY

FRED

TORTOISE

BUSHYTAIL

BUCK TOOTH

BEAKY

MEEK MOUSE

WISE OWL

BILLY GOAT

BONGO

CHIMP

ROBINSON

RAMBLER

RIBBON

BLUEY

SPINNER

BUZZ BEE

ZIP

ROBBIE

DODGER

HENRY

CROCK

JAMES

GUZZLER

PAINTY

BIM

BAM

BOOM

FRANZ

BLACKWING

PAPERETTE   **SCRAP**

PANDA

MR. DOLLAR

OZZY OSTRICH

KEN KANGAROO

PINOCCHIO

GERRY

THE LADYBUGS AND SEVENDOT

MINA   **TINA**   **NINA**

RHINO   **MRS. RHINO**

LIONSTEIN

SNIFFY MOUSE

TOUGH CAT

FROG

CAMEL

SAM

TROOPER

TIP TAP

SKUNK

JUMPING JACK

SLOWCOACH

DROWSY DORMOUSE

HERBERT HOUND

HOTSPUR   MRS. HEN

FLUFFY
FLIP   FLOP

MR. BUNNIKINS   MRS. BUNNIKINS

JOE CROW

WINNIE WHALE

PARDY

OLLY OCTOPUS
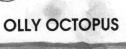

ATTILA

OSCAR

PRICKLES

Another bear thought, "Perhaps I could write some exciting adventures for our new friends." She sat down at grandmother's old typewriter and set to work.

Meanwhile, some other bears had gone exploring. In an old warehouse they found an abandoned printing press. "Why don't we make our very own book using our pictures and stories?" suggested one bear. And that is just what they did.

By early next morning, they had finished their book : The Teddy Bears'
Dictionary. When grandmother awoke she couldn't believe her eyes !

Not only did she have a beautiful teddy bear for each of her
grandchildren but for each one there was also a special Teddy Bears' Dictionary !

THE TEDDY BEARS' DICTIONARY

Text : Pattrick Hudson
Muriel Crawford

Editor : Angela Rahaniotis

Typesetting and Layout : ZAPP

THE TEDDY BEARS' DICTIONARY

Illustrations by Tony Wolf

BRIMAR

© DAMI EDITORE, Italy
© 1991 Brimar Publishing Inc.
338 St. Antoine St. East
Montreal, Canada   H2Y 1A3
Tel. (514) 954-1441
Fax (514) 954-1443

ISBN 2-920845-61-6

Printed in Canada, bound in U.S.A.

Aa

Aa

ABANDON

Everybody but the Captain has **abandoned** ship.

ADVANTAGE

Being tall has its **advantages**.

ABOUT

Buzz Bee finds a painting **about** something he loves.

AFRAID

Even Dr. Spotty is **afraid** of the dentist.

AFTER

Piglet, before... and **after**... his bath.

AGILE

Zip is not nearly as strong as Jumbo, but he is a lot more **agile**.

AGAIN

The Mouse Sisters are such good cooks, visitors come back **again** and **again**.

AGREE

The bunny family all **agree**. Mrs. Bunnikins makes the best carrot stew.

AIM

Piglet **aimed** perfectly but the target ducked...

SUPERSONIC JET

JUMBO JET

GLIDER

HOT AIR BALLOON

MILITARY JET

LIGHT AIRCRAFT

AIRSHIP

TURBO-PROP ENGINES

FUSELAGE

RUDDER

PILOTS

UNDERCARRIAGE

RADAR

RADIO BEACON

WIND SLEEVE

HANGAR

Get out of the way Von Fox!
You haven't been given
permission to land.

RADAR

APRON

RUNWAY LIGHTS

PASSENGER BRIDGE

CONTROL TOWER

RUNWAY

AMBULANCE AND FIRE ENGINE

HELICOPTER

TERMINAL

ALTHOUGH

Although Herbert is hot on the trail, he doesn't have a clue whose footprints these are.

ALWAYS

Billy Goat was **always** told not to play with matches. Now he knows why.

AMAZING

Prickles thinks he looks **amazing** with his new punk haircut.

AMOUNT

Henry asked for the bill, but when he saw the **amount**, he fainted.

ANGRY

When Mrs. Bunnikins is **angry**, Mr. Bunnikins puts in his earplugs even if it's his fault.

ANOTHER

"Officer, I was only trying to..." but PC Stop does not want to hear **another** excuse.

ANY

Tortoise didn't waste **any** time delivering Skunk's parcel.

ANYONE

There doesn't seem to be **anyone** for miles !

APPRECIATE

Lionstein **appreciates** music except when it is played by Bim, Bam, and Boom.

APPROVE

Dr. Spotty doesn't **approve** of Joe Crow smoking in his waiting room.

APOLOGIZE

When water's dripping through the floor, and flowing out your neighbor's door, even if he's twice your size, it's best to go **apologize**.

ARCHITECTURE

APARTMENT BUILDING

CHALET

ROW HOUSES

CASTLE

SKYSCRAPER

COTTAGE

FACTORY

CHURCH

MANSION

Prickles asked an **architect** to design his new house. He's not sure what type of house it is. Do you know?

Is a cat **as** fast **as** a mouse is quick?

ASHAMED

Attila is so **ashamed**. His pants fell down and everyone saw his polka-dot shorts.

a 21

ASTRONAUT

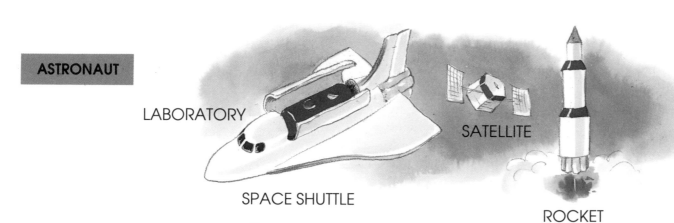

LABORATORY

SPACE SHUTTLE

SATELLITE

ROCKET

Von Fox would love to be the first fox **astronaut** in space.

ASTRONOMY

PLANETS TRAVEL AROUND THE SUN.

EARTH

SUN

THE MOON TRAVELS AROUND THE EARTH.

Astronomy is the science of the stars and planets. Lionstein is an astronomer. He thought he had discovered a new planet, until Sevendot flew away from the end of his telescope.

AVALANCHE

Jumbo caused an **avalanche** when he tried to ski.

AWAY

Robinson thought an iceberg could be his ship to cross the shining sea, but as the sun warmed the day, his boat began to melt **away**.

AWFUL

Chimp thinks he's **awfully** funny, but Trooper doesn't.

Bb

BARBER

BACK

Ozzy left a note saying "**back** soon" so that he could go for a ride on Tiger's new motorcycle.

BAFFLE

Lionstein is **baffled**. Now how will he finish the problem ?

BACKPACK

"I'm going to bring a smaller **backpack** next time," Franz promises himself.

BANG

Bim **banged** his drum a little too hard.

BANKRUPT

Mr. Dollar is hiding from his clients because his bank has gone **bankrupt**. Where did he spend all of the money ?

BARBER

The **barber** is afraid that Guzzler doesn't like his haircut.

BECAUSE

The meeting ended suddenly **because** Skunk walked in.

BARGAIN

"Three bones for a dollar is a great **bargain**," says Timmy.

BEHIND

Attila is happy to stay **behind** and let Jumbo clear a path through the snow.

BELIEVE

No one can **believe** that Timmy wants a dollar for three bones.

BESIDE

Frog finished his work early so he could sit **beside** the lake and relax.

BEST

Math is not Teddy's **best** subject.

BETTER

Teddy is much **better** at drawing.

BLAME

Rusty will get **blamed** for making fun of Wise Owl.

BLOCK

Von Fox stopped to buy a paper. Now he's **blocking** traffic.

BLOW

Birdie's house was **blown** down.
It is time to move.

BOND

I'd like us to form a special **bond**...
Will you marry me ?

BOISTEROUS

The pupils are a little **boisterous** during art class.

BOOK

Teddy would like to write a **book**.
But he can't think of the first sentence.

BOLD

A beautiful cake placed on the ledge
by a mouse with a heart of gold.
"No one would ever take my cake,
no one would be that **bold**."

BORING

Lionstein's speech is so **boring** that everyone
except Dr. Spotty has left.

TREES

FIR
BANANA
COCONUT PALM
BIRCH
OAK
POPLAR
BEECH

FLOWERS

ROSE
IRIS
VIOLET
TULIP
FORGET-ME-NOT
DAISY
BUTTERCUP

FRUITS

APPLE
PEAR
CHERRIES
STRAWBERRY
FIG
ORANGE
WALNUT
CHESTNUT
WATERMELON
PLUM
GRAPES

VEGETABLES

CAULIFLOWER
PEAS
TOMATO
EGGPLANT
ONION
CELERY
CARROT
TURNIP
POTATO

Of all the plants that Fluffy studies in **botany** class, his favorite is...

BOUNCE

Jumping Jack didn't know he had been placed under the stairs when he **bounced** out of his box.

BRAKE

On steep hills, the Captain uses his **brakes** *and* an anchor.

BOW

Mr. Dollar is Crock's best customer. Whenever he comes in, Crock greets him with a deep **bow**.

BRANCH

"Herbert ! You're sawing the wrong end of the **branch** !"

BOX

Nine **boxes**, one candy... someone's played a joke on Crock.

BRAY

Everyone wishes that
Dunk would stop **braying**.

BREAK

When Henry Hippo **broke** through the ice,
they needed a crane to lift him out.

BREAST STROKE

After Henry broke through the ice, Frog
decided to teach everyone the **breast stroke**.

BUNCH

Chimp is trying to figure out
how many **bunches** of bananas he ate.

BUTLER

In the Teddy Bears'
Dictionary, James
is the **butler.**

CHEF

Cc

CHEF

CACTUS

A **cactus** is Sniffy's favorite plant. Tough Cat, however, doesn't like them at all.

CAGE

Guzzler is a pest, so he's been shut in a special steel **cage**.

CALCULATE

5, 6, 7, 8
What a way
to **calculate**!

JANUARY

1

On January 1st, there is snow everywhere up north. Robinson decides to go visit his friends who live in warmer places.

31

FEBRUARY

1

Through cold February, he drives south on Wally's sleigh.

28

MARCH

1

In March, strong winds make it easier for Robinson to travel by sailcart.

31

APRIL

1

In April, Robinson visits Painty but it is always raining so he moves on.

30

MAY

1

In May, summer is just around the corner. Robinson hops a ride with Ken.

31

JUNE

1

In June, it is warm and sunny. Robinson spends the month playing with Fluffy.

30

JULY

1

July is a hot month. Robinson decides to visit Frog at the beach and spend the month swimming.

31

AUGUST

1

In August it is also very hot. Robinson is on his way to visit another friend but he always has time to stop for an ice cream.

31

SEPTEMBER

1

In September, farmers are starting to take things to market so Robinson rides along.

30

OCTOBER

1

In October, Robinson gets lost so the Ladybugs help him find his way home before it gets too cold.

31

NOVEMBER

1

Almost home, Robinson strolls through the falling leaves and thinks about all of the friends he visited.

30

DECEMBER

1

Finally, in the last month of the year, Robinson sees his warm house again and is glad because in December, it is very cold.

31

CAVITY

Bacteria love to make **cavities** in your teeth. They hate toothbrushes.

CHANCE

Quite by **chance**, Mrs. Bunnikins and Mrs. Piggles have bought the same hat.

CHOIR

A ladybug that sings
is something to admire;
fifteen singing all at once
now that's a special **choir**.

CHAT

Mrs. Hen loves to **chat** with her friends.

CHORE

When you have to carry your house on your back, going uphill is a real **chore** !

CHRISTMAS

It's **Christmas** ! Can you tell whose presents are under the tree ?

CHUBBY

Henry likes being **chubby**.
It helps him stay afloat.

CHUNK

Henry Hippo has cut the cake in two pieces.
Who do you think will get the bigger **chunk** ?

CIRCLE

Ribbon doesn't need a geometry set.
She can draw a **circle** all by herself.

Teddy is an acrobat,
Meek Mouse is a clown.
There's fun for everyone today,
the **circus** is in town.

CLASS

Today the teacher's showing how to write the letter G.
Flip knows that spelling's not art **class** though that's where he'd rather be.

CLAW

Mrs. Blackwing thinks that it is very stylish to paint her **claws** bright red.

CLEAN

Olly is a **clean** fiend !

CLIMB

Bandit didn't quite make a clean getaway when he **climbed** over the gate to escape from PC Stop.

CLUB

THE GRAND WEB CLUB
"Free Admission"

Spinner is gloomy. Nobody wants to join his **club**.

COLLABORATE

The Teddy Brothers **collaborated** in making this book. It was fun to work together.

COLLIDE

Von Fox nearly **collided** with Blackwing.
He only missed by a feather.

COMFORT

Fluffy had a nightmare so Mummy
gave him a big kiss to **comfort** him.

COMB

Rusty has invented an adjustable **comb**.
Only Guzzler is afraid to try it.

COME

SHAMROCK INC.

When Tiger's truck **came** to a sudden stop,
everyone else did too.

A **compass** always points north so polar bears can never get lost.

CONCEAL

Rusty **concealed** his failing mark by putting a "1" in front of the "0".

CONGRATULATE

Daddy Fox **congratulates** Rusty on getting top marks. How did he manage it?

CONCENTRATE

CONNECT

Oscar should switch off the electricity before he **connects** the wires.

Lawyer Bear **concentrates** very hard when he writes — even when he writes to his Mom.

COURSE

Teddy is trying to warn the Captain
to change **course**.

CROSSROAD

Zip couldn't make up his mind which way to go
when he came to the **crossroad**.

CROWD

Everyone **crowds** around to listen
to the Captain's adventures.

CUSTOMER

Henry's telling his **customer** that the hat
suits him perfectly.

CUT

Jumbo and Rhino are fighting over the same
scarf. If they don't **cut** it out, Meek Mouse will.

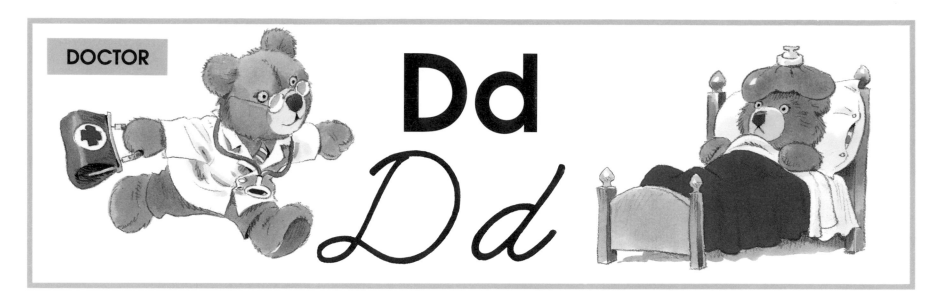

DOCTOR

Dd
Dd

DANCER

What a graceful **dancer** you are, Henry !

DASH

When Bulldog is angry, it is better to **dash** off than ask him why.

DECIDE

Poor Meek Mouse ! When he **decided** to ask Matilda to marry him, she ran away.

DECORATE

Piglet's **decorating** the Christmas tree. His ancestor was **decorated** for bravery in battle.

DEFEND

Even the bees have to **defend** their home from Bandit.

Ice melts quickly
when you live in the
desert.

Joe Crow is very, very nosey.
Here he is reading Violet's secret **diary**.

DIFFERENCE

At the end of the match,
Henry doesn't know which team
he's supposed to give the trophy to...

The players are all so muddy,
he can't tell the **difference**
between the winners and
the losers.

DIGEST

Dinner is ready, but Henry's sound asleep.
He's still **digesting** his heavy lunch.

DISAPPOINT

Painty is very **disappointed**. Paperette ran
away crying when she saw her portrait.

DISCOVER

Crafty Herbert is about to **discover**
who's been cycling on the grass.

DISGUISE

Who stole the apples ?
Herbert has found the perfect
disguise to help him catch
the thief.

DISINFECTANT

"Amazing," says Piglet.
"This **disinfectant** doesn't sting."

DISOBEDIENT

Fluffy is not really **disobedient**.
Daddy told him to wake him up at 3 o'clock.

DOSE

"Oh no," thinks Ozzy, "maybe I should have taken only one **dose** of feather syrup."

DOWN

Tiger needs a new job.
He can't look **down**
or he'll get dizzy.

DOUBT

Sniffy **doubts**
that Tough Cat can be nice,
but that cheese looks so good
he'd really like a slice.

DRAMATIC

In the desert, people do **dramatic**
things to get a bit of shade.

DRAW

After the double knockout,
the referee shouts
"It's a **draw**!"

DREAM

This is James' favorite **dream**.

DRIVE

Zip was so busy saying "hello", that he **drove** into a lamppost.

DROP

"**Drop** the curtain! **Drop** the curtain!" thinks Oscar. "I don't want to be a star any more!"

DUO

Flip and Flop are known as the "dynamic **duo**" of the class. They are both always ready with the answer.

Ee

EARLY

Slowcoach was going to be late, but with Tortoise's help, maybe now he'll arrive **early**.

ECHO

"Where are you Franz?" shouted Franz.
"Where are you Fraaannzzz?" replied his **echo**.

EARN

Painty **earned** a lot of money for painting Mr. Dollar's portrait.

ECLIPSE

When the moon covers the sun, it is called an **eclipse**. Don't worry though, the sun comes back in a few minutes.

ECOLOGY

THE WORLD IS BEAUTIFUL
AND IT BELONGS TO EVERYONE.
HELP US TO KEEP IT THAT WAY!

Panda and the Teddies are making a banner for **ecology** day.

EDGE

Mr. Piggles and Piglet are placing stakes
at the **edge** of their giant carrot garden.

EDUCATED

You have to be well **educated** to
be the king of beasts.

EDITOR

I'm the **editor** of this dictionary.
If you find any mistakes, phone 777-BEAR.

EFFORT

All of Mr. Piggles' **efforts** have paid off.
This year his carrots are gigantic!

ELEGANT

Beaky's sure he's going to be the most **elegant** guest at the party!

END

Sevendot is waiting for Ribbon to pop out of the **end** of the tube.

ENERGY

Drowsy Dormouse didn't have enough **energy** to finish the race, so he took a quick nap.

EMERGENCY

Von Fox has had to make an **emergency** landing.

ENTANGLE

Your root beer is safe Franz. Von Fox is **entangled** on the sign.

EMPTY

Meek Mouse invited Olly out to lunch. After he paid the bill, his pockets are **empty**.

ENTRANCE

Oh no, the packages are blocking Mrs. Bunnikins' view and Jumbo is blocking the **entrance**.

ERROR

Somebody should tell Painty he's made an **error**. Do you know what it is ?

TO ERR IS HUMAN

Anyone can make **errors** !

ETCETERA

Onedot Ladybug has one spot on his back, Twodot has two spots, Threedot has three, **etcetera, etcetera, etcetera.**

EVEN

Even with two thick sweaters, Mrs. Hen is still cold.

EVERY

Paperette is upset.
Every time she erases the marks from her dress, Scrap writes on her again.

EXCITEMENT

Prickles goes wild with **excitement** when his team scores.

FARMER

F f **Ff**

FARM

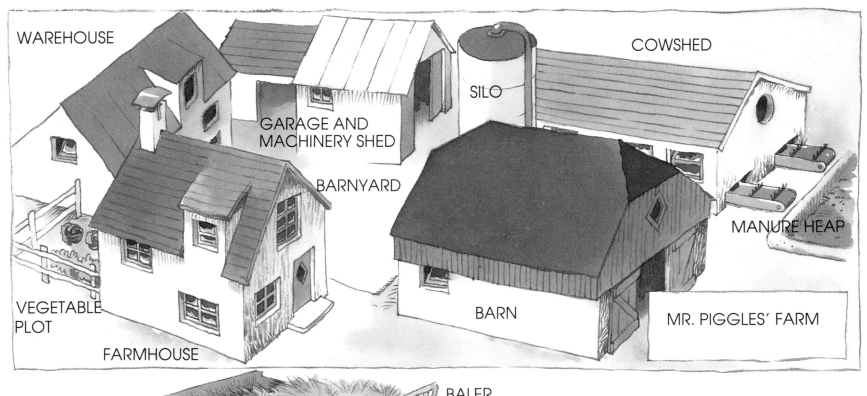

WAREHOUSE

GARAGE AND
MACHINERY SHED

SILO

COWSHED

BARNYARD

MANURE HEAP

VEGETABLE
PLOT

BARN

MR. PIGGLES' FARM

FARMHOUSE

BALER

COMBINE HARVESTER

SOWING MACHINE

TRACTOR

PLOUGH

SHEARS SPRAYER WATERING CAN SCYTHE SICKLE

PITCH FORK

RAKE

SPADE SHOVEL HOE

SPRINKLER

Piggles is a very good **farmer**!
These are the tools he uses in the fields.

FAR-SIGHTED

Winter's a long way off, but **far-sighted**
Bushytail is busily storing nuts!

FASHION

Blue feathers
are the height
of **fashion** this
year.

FAR WEST

INDIAN
CHIEF

TRAPPER

COWBOY

SHERIFF

PONY EXPRESS
RIDER

CAVALRYMAN GOLD PROSPECTOR

If Teddy lived in the **Far West**, he'd like to be a...

FAULT

Robbie is now walking upside down.
Whose **fault** is that ?

FAVORITE

Robbie's **favorite**
book is "The Robot
Maintenance Manual".

FEATURE

Pinocchio's most noticeable
feature is his...

FIGHT

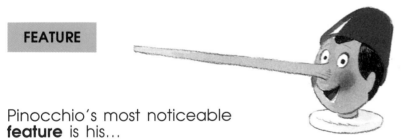

Attila has a black eye today.
"Who have you been **fighting** with ?"
Billy Goat asks him.

FINISH

Teddy is making a list of friends in this book
whose names **finish** with "y".
Why don't you help him ?

FIRST

It's better to wipe your feet **first**
than wash the floor later !

FIT

Olly Octopus has eight arms.
That's why he can never find
a sweater to **fit** him.

FIX

Zip is sure to win the race now
that he's **fixed** up his car.

FLAG

PENNANT

WEATHER VANE

SIGNAL FLAGS

NATIONAL FLAGS

A black and white **flag** with skull and crossbones is the **flag** of a pirate ship.

FOOTPRINT

All Joe Crow wanted to do was leave his **footprints** in the wet cement. Now he's stuck!

FOR

"A parcel! I hope it's **for** me," says Sam.

FORCE

The Mouse Sisters don't like litter. They **force** Bongo to pick up the banana peel he threw away.

FORMAL

Crock, James and Oscar have been invited to a **formal** party. It's a black-and-white affair.

FROM

Mrs. Bunnikins marked Flip so that she could tell him apart **from** Flop.

FRACAS

What a **fracas** !
And it all began with two bunnies.

FULL

At night, Attila can usually be heard howling at the **full** moon.

FRIGHT

The first time Frog saw Guzzler, he got such a **fright** his legs shook.

FUTURE

"I see dozens of eggs in your **future**..."

Gg

Gg (cursive)

GADGET

Violet's new **gadget** will make delicious ice cream.

GALLOP

Teddy **gallops** away on his white steed.

GAME

Sevendot is explaining a new **game**. It starts with the Ladybugs in a circle hopping on one leg.

GASP

Tiger won't be **gasping** for air on this job.

GEAR

Zip can't get the car into **gear**. Let's hope he doesn't put it into reverse.

GENERALLY

The Captain knows that, **generally**, the calmest waters are behind a sleeping whale.

GENEROUS

Mr. Dollar is not very **generous** with his money. He is a miser.

GENTLE

GENIUS

"If you're such a **genius**," says Robbie, "figure this out."

Oscar's head is very sore because while going to the store, the **gentle** breeze that cooled the day sent a flowerpot his way.

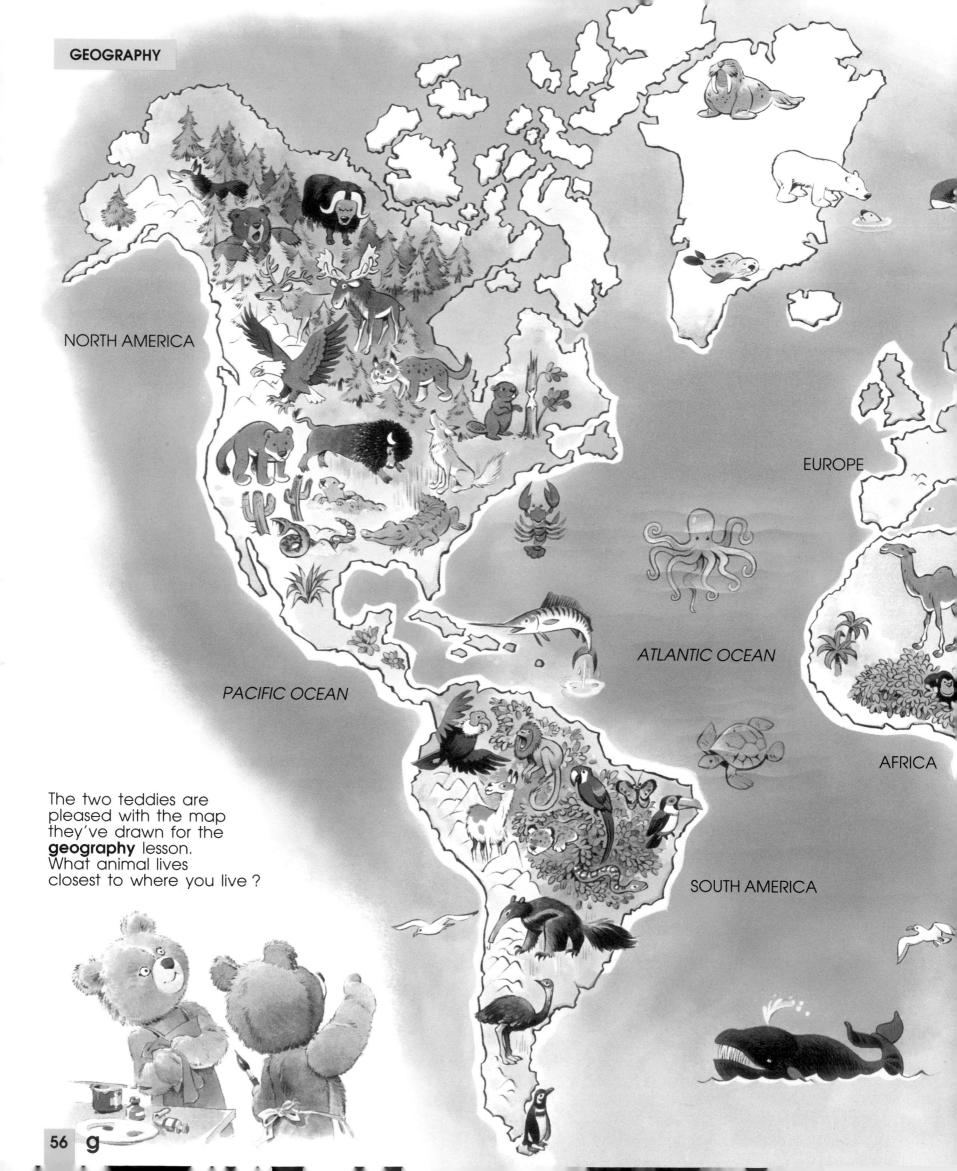

NORTH AMERICA

EUROPE

ATLANTIC OCEAN

PACIFIC OCEAN

AFRICA

The two teddies are pleased with the map they've drawn for the **geography** lesson. What animal lives closest to where you live?

SOUTH AMERICA

ARCTIC OCEAN

ASIA

PACIFIC OCEAN

INDIAN OCEAN

AUSTRALIA

GET

This is all the lunch Henry is **getting** today.
He is on a diet.

GHASTLY

"What a pretty hat!" exclaims Mrs. Piggles
(thinks "really **ghastly**").

GIANT

Sevendot sprinkled his flower with magic water
and it grew into a **giant** daisy.

GIVE

"If he doesn't **give** me some bones,
I'll never speak to him again!"

GLARE

PC **glares** at Bandit.
Will that stop him from stealing the apple?

GLASSES

"So that's where I put my **glasses**!"
says Lionstein.

GLOBE

Sam's favorite class is geography because he gets to spin the **globe**.

GOLD

Dodger swears he collects **gold**. Everyone else swears he steals it.

GOOD

Before the teacher went out, she said to her pupils: "Be **good**."

GOSSIP

Henny told Penny a secret.
Penny told Betty and Betty told Milly.
That's how **gossip** gets around.

GRAND

Mrs. Rhino made a **grand** entrance at the
ambassador's ball.

GRANDAD

Henry Hippo boasts that his **grandad** was a
famous ballet dancer, but nobody believes him.

GRATEFUL

Timmy is **grateful** that Tommy let him
share his house.

GREAT

Bushytail and Gerry are the **greatest** of friends.
They see things eye to eye.

GUEST

An unexpected **guest** arrived
in the middle of the night.
That's just like Robinson !

HOSTESS

Hh

Hh

HAMMER

Chimp tried to **hammer** a nail into the wall,
but he missed.

HAPPY

Jumping Jack is **happy**.
Someone has finally opened his box.

HANDLEBARS

Pinocchio thought he'd leave the road
to stay away from cars,
but when his bike hit a bump
he only had his **handlebars**.

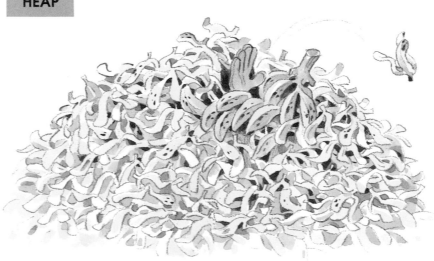

HEAP

Bongo or Chimp has eaten a **heap** of bananas.
Guess who ?

HELICOPTER

Pardy has wanted to fly **helicopters** ever since he was little.

HELP

Is a visit to Dr. Spotty going to **help** Robbie much ?

HERE

Can you guess who had lunch **here** ?

HIDE

Chimp thought he'd better **hide** after he took Bongo's bananas.

HIGH

"Yes, you look much better wearing a **high**-necked shirt !"

HONEY

Teddy would love some **honey** but...

HOORAY!

Every time Tip Tap does his little dance, the audience cheers "**Hooray**!"

HOP

Pardy is too close to the powerlines and Frog is **hopping** about warning him of the danger.

HOPE

Sniffy sure **hopes** he can get his tail free.

HORN

Billy Goat usually has his **horns** polished, but he doesn't often trim his beard.

HORRIBLE

"You're a **horrible** cat!" wails Sniffy.

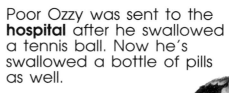

HOSPITAL

Poor Ozzy was sent to the **hospital** after he swallowed a tennis ball. Now he's swallowed a bottle of pills as well.

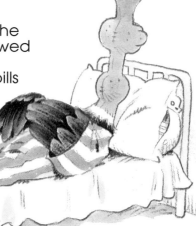

HOUSE

Henry's sneeze hit the **house** of cards like a tornado.

HUNGRY

Whenever Olly is **hungry**, he's glad he has eight arms.

HOWEVER

Attila's pants are too big for him. **However**, he is sure to grow into them.

HUNTING

Panda says: "People who go **hunting** don't love animals."

HUMOR

Bongo does not see the **humor** in Chimp's silly tricks.

HURRY

This is the fastest way to **hurry** down the stairs. It is also the fastest way to get into trouble.

ICE CREAM MAN

Ii

Ii

ICE HOCKEY

As usual, in **ice hockey**,
the only person not fighting
has the puck.

ICICLE

An **icicle** is nature's winter treat.

IDEA

Tiger's headlight isn't working, but Robbie had a bright **idea**.

IMAGINE

Sniffy likes to **imagine** that he is twice as big as Tough Cat.

IMMEDIATELY

A BALDY'S PARADISE
MAGIC LOTION

Joe Crow sells magic hair lotion. Rusty **immediately** discovers that it's a trick.

ILLUSTRATION

Everyone loves the **illustrations** in this book.

IMPORTANT

It is very **important** to check where you put an open flame.

INHERIT

Mr. Dollar's nephews will probably **inherit** a lot of money one day. They also **inherited** large feet and strong beaks.

INCONVENIENT

It's very **inconvenient** to have a giraffe sit in front of you at the cinema.

INSIDE

Robbie would love to go swimming too, but he'll rust if he gets his **insides** wet.

INSIST

Trooper **insists** that the castle is closed today.

INDEED

Seven times as many legs means seven times the speed. The Ladybugs are very fast, very fast **indeed**.

INSPIRE

Crafty Herbert's cases have **inspired** Beaky to write a detective novel.

INSTANT

Jumbo plugs his ears the **instant** he sees Bim, Bam, and Boom.

INTERESTING

What could it be that the Captain finds so **interesting** ?

INTERRUPT

Joe Crow **interrupts** Mr. Bunnikins to ask the time.

INTIMATE

Jumbo has interrupted the Piggles **intimate** family dinner.

INTO

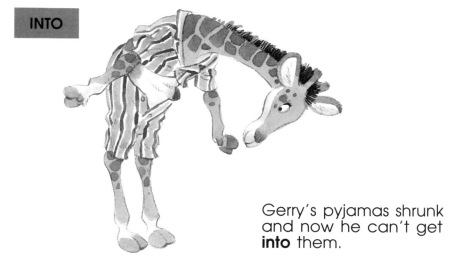

Gerry's pyjamas shrunk and now he can't get **into** them.

INVENT

Spinner hopes that he has **invented** a way to attract more bees.

An **irritating** noise woke up prickles;
it's Drowsy Dormouse snoring.

"Where's the ship to leave the **island** ?" thinks
Robinson. "They said it was down at the beach."

JUDGE

Jj

That **jacket** Oscar's trying on is much too tight.
It wouldn't fit a pigeon.

Beaky isn't always sure
there's truth to Bandit's tale,
but as his lawyer, it's his job
to keep him out of **jail**.

JOB

Lionstein has asked Robbie to add up all of the numbers in the phone book. What a **job**!

JOIN

Jumbo and Meek Mouse **join** forces to launch the Captain's new boat.

JOKE

Meek Mouse has just told what he thought was a funny **joke** about elephants but no one's laughing.

JOSTLE

Rhino has the worst habit of **jostling** people to get ahead of the line.

JUMP

Tip Tap needs to practice his long **jump**.

JUST

Gerry can't swim, so he brought a floater or two... **just** in case...

Kk

K k

KINDERGARTEN TEACHER

KANGAROO

Ken is showing off again
with all that he can do.
"If someone else can do it," says Ken,
"then so can a **kangaroo**!"

KEEN

Everyone is **keen** to hear all about
Robinson's travels.

KICK

What a great **kick**! Even Olly couldn't stop it.

k 71

KIND

Isn't it **kind** of Bongo to lighten Chimp's load?

KNACK

Mr. Dollar has a **knack** for making money.

KNIT

Olly may end up wearing his sweater before he finishes **knitting** it.

KNOCK

Mr. Bunnikins doesn't know where all of the **knocking** is coming from. "Everyone must be hanging up pictures today," he thinks.

KNOT

While they were sleeping, Chimp tied Ribbon and Crock's tail in a **knot**.

KNOW

Teddy's so polite he even says "good morning" to people he doesn't **know**.

Ll

LIBRARIAN

LAKE

As far as Tip Tap is concerned,
a dish of water is a **lake**.

LANGUAGE

What **language** is that, Robbie?
It does not look like English.

LASSO

Cowboy Teddy has **lassoed** poor Dunk.

LAST

Piglet's lucky. He won't
have to climb the tree
to get the **last** apple.

Frog is **late** for school again.

It's easy for Robbie to be right-handed or **left-handed**.

LAW

Bandit is forever breaking the **law**.

LEGS

Bandit needs a fast pair of **legs** when he goes "shopping" for grapes.

LEARN

The students were quick to **learn** their lesson on how airplanes fly.

LEAST

"Can't we at **least** stop and talk to Crock ?" asks Fluffy.

LICK

Licking your plate may not be polite, but it sure tastes good.

LIGHTNING

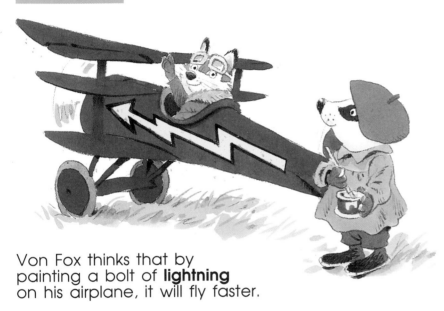

Von Fox thinks that by painting a bolt of **lightning** on his airplane, it will fly faster.

LIMP

Mr. Piggles is **limping** because he hit his toes with the hoe.

LINGER

During his voyages, Robinson sometimes finds a place where he likes to **linger** (stay awhile).

LIQUID

Water is a **liquid**. You can float in it.

When the weather is cold, it turns into ice and becomes a solid.

When it's warm again, the ice melts into water.

LINE

Ribbon can make a straight **line**... a wavy **line**... or zigzags.

Tiger is **listening** to the engine. Rhino says
his car has been making funny noises.

LIVE

This is where Tip Tap **lives**.
He thinks his home is his castle.

LOAN

Banker Bear is surprised. Slowcoach is
asking for a bank **loan** to buy a bigger house.

LOAD

Dunk thinks that the **load** is too heavy.

LOCK

"No **lock** is too big when you want
to protect your best things," thinks James.

LOCOMOTIVE

Fluffy's **locomotive** broke down. The Ladybugs are pushing it to the station.

LODGE

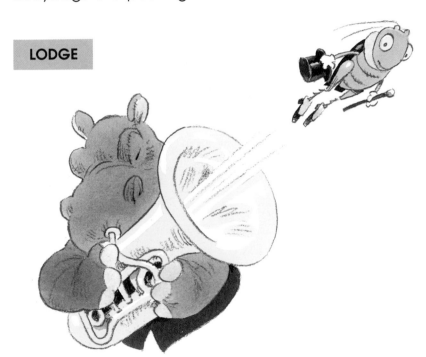

Something was **lodged** in Henry's trombone. It's gone now !

LOOK

Mrs. Bunnikins has asked Dad to **look** after the twins while she's out.

LONELY

Without Flop, Flip thinks marbles is the **loneliest** game in the world.

LOOSE

"Please Tiger, will you check me ? My friends say I've got a screw **loose**."

Mm

MILKMAN

MACARONI

Meek Mouse is helping the Mouse Sisters make **macaroni**.

MAGIC

Magic lets you take birds out of a hat.
Let's hope it lets you put them back in as well.

MAIL

Scrap and Paperette are going to visit friends by air **mail**.

MAKE

MAGNIFYING GLASS

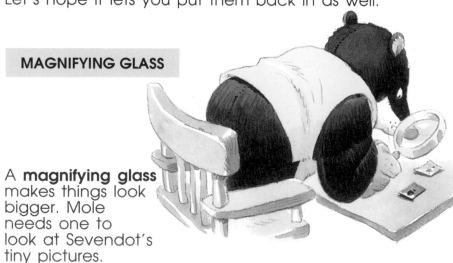

A **magnifying glass** makes things look bigger. Mole needs one to look at Sevendot's tiny pictures.

Mr. Dollar **made** his fortune selling fridges in the North Pole.

MAKEUP

Mrs. Rhino is wearing so much **makeup** that her husband doesn't recognize her.

MARVELLOUS

"Wouldn't it be **marvellous** to lose a few pounds?" sighs Mrs. Rhino.

MANNERS

"Remember your **manners**," say the Ladybugs. "We have a guest for dinner."

MAP

Mole can't believe it.
The **map** led him to an empty treasure chest.

MASKED

Can you guess who is at the **masked** ball?

MARMALADE

Teddy has eaten all the **marmalade** and now he has a tummyache.

MAYBE

Olly's looking for a tennis partner.
Maybe he'll have trouble finding one!

MAZE

Can you help Flip find his way through the **maze** and reach Fluffy ?

MEANS

Olly Octopus uses eight tennis racquets, which **means** he can play many people at once.

MELON

"Bongo, that's not the way to choose ripe **melons**!"

MESSAGE

The Captain is sending a **message** for help.

MIMIC

Sniffy's trying to **mimic** Tough Cat's growl.

MIND

Crock doesn't **mind** if Dr. Spotty looks at Jumbo's broken tusk first.
He feels silly about having bitten his tongue.

MISTAKE

What a silly **mistake**! Threedot said "hello" to Fourdot, thinking he was Fivedot!

MIXTURE

What a revolting **mixture**!
Is this Robbie's idea of helping in the kitchen?

MONSTER

Guzzler is furious because everyone keeps telling him he's a **monster**.
Maybe it's true.

MOOD

Jumbo broke his leg skiing.
Now he's in a terrible **mood**.

MOST

PC Stop is not like **most** people.
He likes motor oil on his shoulders.

MORE

If you're not sure who
weighs **more**, a see-saw
will help you find out.

MORNING

Olly has a hearty breakfast every **morning**.

MUCH

Gerry **much** prefers the middle
of the sandwich to the crust.

NURSE

Nn

$\mathcal{N}\mathit{n}$

NAKED

Scrap is as **naked** as the day he was snipped out of a blank sheet of paper.

NAUGHTY

Naughty Chimp waited until Bongo was asleep before he made off with one of his bananas.

NAP

The opera is the perfect place for Drowsy Dormouse to take a **nap**.

NEARLY

NASTY

Joe Crow is telling Crock that it is **nasty** to say he has a big nose. His isn't so small either.

Flip and Flop were sick. It looks like they're **nearly** better now!

Mole swears he doesn't **need** glasses !

Spinner thought a big long **net**
would catch more than a fly,
but when he found it was Guzzler he caught,
he thought that he would cry.

"I don't understand," thinks the Captain,
"my ships **never** sink in the bathtub."

At long last, Robinson has returned from his
travels. "What's **new** ?" he asks.

Meek Mouse has missed the bus,
so he is hurrying to the **next** stop.

"Have a **nice** lunch !"
"Thanks ! The same to you !"

NO

After drawing the **no** smoking sign, Teddy is now putting it into place.

NOT

Not even a marching band can wake up Drowsy Dormouse.

NOBODY

Everyone knows that **nobody** is allowed to smoke in the cinema. Now Joe Crow knows too.

NOTHING

James always thought that **nothing** would ever frighten him.

NORTH

Sam and Wally pop out of the water; "Fancy meeting you at the **North** Pole !"

NOTICE

Oh, oh, too late ! Crock didn't **notice** the "Wet Paint" sign.

OFFICER

Oo

Oo

OBEY

Teddy is **obeying** the doctor's orders. He is rubbing ointment on the spot where he hit his head.

OBVIOUS

"It is **obvious** that you will not change," says the judge. "Forty days without bubble gum!"

OCCASION

OBSERVE

Guzzler is **observing** the candle. As soon as it goes out, he'll eat it.

Rambler keeps his best suit for special **occasions**!

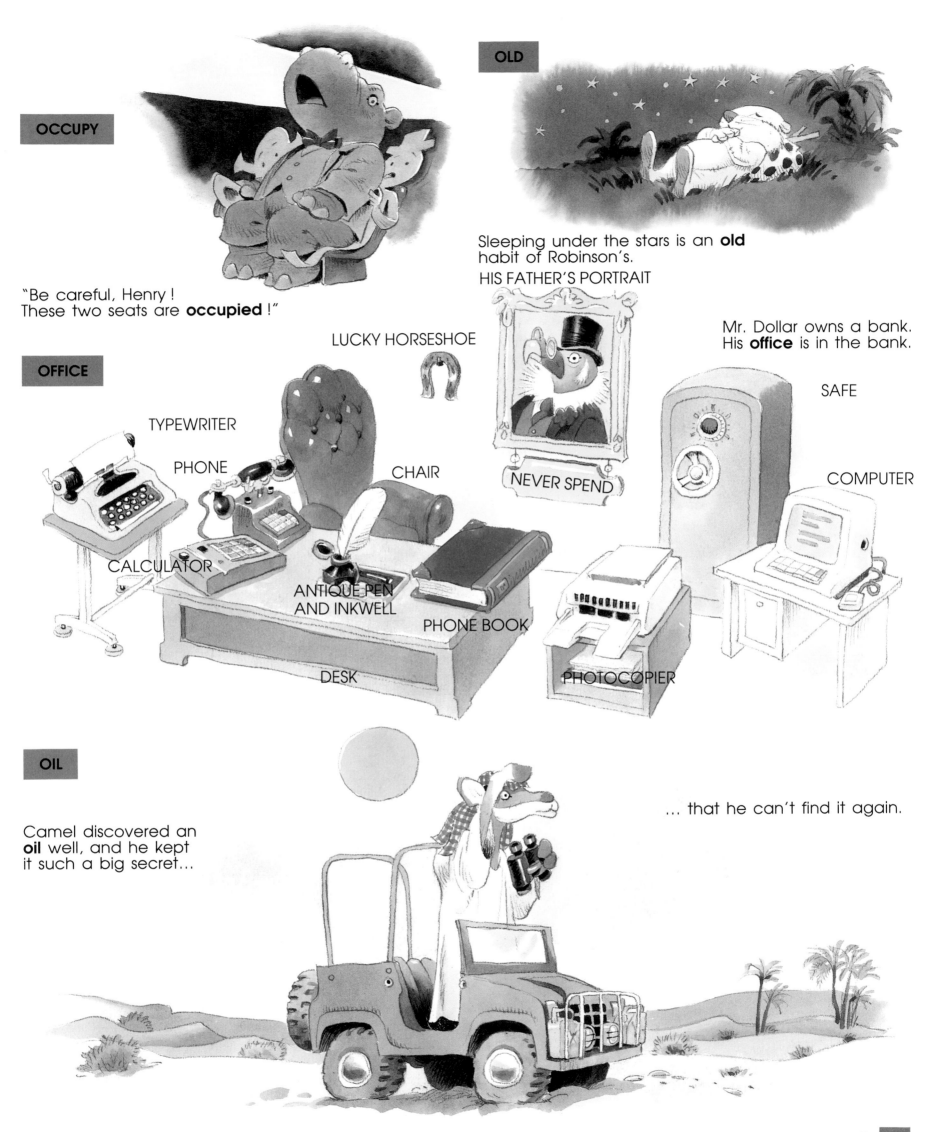

OCCUPY

"Be careful, Henry !
These two seats are **occupied** !"

OLD

Sleeping under the stars is an **old**
habit of Robinson's.

HIS FATHER'S PORTRAIT

Mr. Dollar owns a bank.
His **office** is in the bank.

LUCKY HORSESHOE

OFFICE

SAFE

TYPEWRITER

PHONE

CHAIR

NEVER SPEND

COMPUTER

CALCULATOR

ANTIQUE PEN
AND INKWELL

PHONE BOOK

DESK

PHOTOCOPIER

OIL

... that he can't find it again.

Camel discovered an
oil well, and he kept
it such a big secret...

ON

Tip Tap is so talented he can dance **on** his own top hat!

ONE

Drowsy Dormouse has been awake only **one** day this week.

OPEN

Mr. Piggles flings the door **open**, unaware that it's being repainted.

OPINION

Rhino has just given Painty his **opinion** of his portrait!

OPPORTUNITY

As soon as Bongo got his new hammer, he took the **opportunity** to test Fred's helmet.

OPTIMIST

"The bottle's half empty!" declares Meek Mouse, who is a pessimist. "No, it's half full!" replies Rambler, the **optimist**.

ORDER

Panda drew a detour in **order** to save the tree.

ORIGINAL

Pardy has found an **original** way to dry Mrs. Piggles' washing.

OTHER

If Bandit wins at checkers, does he get to go to the **other** side of the bars ?

OUGHT

The barber thinks that Lionstein **ought** to have visited him a long time ago.

OUT

Prickles is sure he could get inside Bluey's house, but he doubts that he could get **out**.

OVERTURN

Frog is seeing if anyone in the **overturned** van needs help.

Pp

PHOTOGRAPHER

PACK

On the way to the parade,
everyone **packed** into one bus.

PAINT

Lionstein has **painted** lines on the walls
and made the world's biggest notebook.

PAIR

PAIN

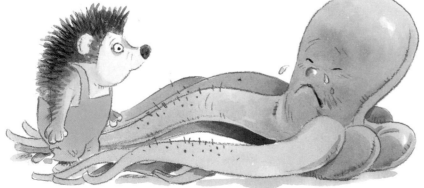

Olly Octopus gets an awful **pain**
after cuddling Prickles !

"I thought you brought the water," says Jumbo.
"I thought you brought the water," says Chimp.
What a fine **pair** these two are.

PAPER

Mr. Bunnikins can't get any peace and quiet to read his **paper**.

PARTNER

Flip ducked and let his soccer **partner** take the penalty.

PASTE

Bongo has **pasted** the poster to himself instead of to the wall.

PEACE

Trooper is a **peace**-loving soldier. **Peace** is good, war is not !

PECULIAR

Guzzler felt very **peculiar** after he ate the soap.

PERFECT

Piglet can't believe it ! A **perfect** shot !

PERFUME

"I'd like a nice delicate **perfume**, please !" says Skunk.

PICK

Violet respects nature so she doesn't **pick** this flower.

PILE

The Ladybugs are faced with a **pile** of dishes to wash. Henry and Jumbo were over for lunch.

PLATE

Guzzler enjoyed the cake so much he's eating the **plate** !

PLEASED

Wally is very **pleased**. These flowers are delicious.

POINT

There's no mistaking which way Chimp is **pointing**.

POLE

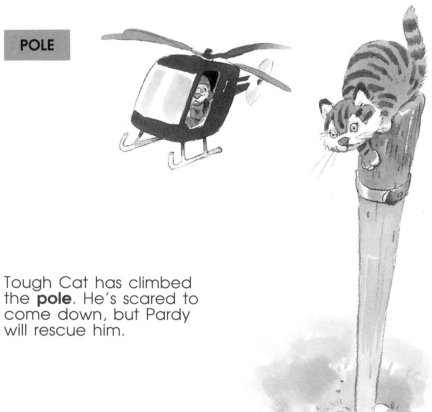

Tough Cat has climbed the **pole**. He's scared to come down, but Pardy will rescue him.

POLITE

It's not **polite** to look over someone's shoulder.

POSTAGE

Paperette is cutting herself a skirt from a **postage** stamp.

PRACTICE

Practice makes for a perfect shot !

POSTCARD

Mole collects **postcards**.
At night, he pretends he is somewhere else.

PREFER

"I'd **prefer** if you didn't squash the flowers !"
says Buzz Bee.

PRESENT

A fluffy bathrobe
is a wonderful **present**.
Scrap is very grateful.

PRETEND

Jumbo's **pretending** to be a zebra,
but he's not fooling anyone.

PRINT

The Teddy Brothers are delighted.
Their dictionary has just been **printed**.

PROMISE

Ozzy **promised** to be good
and take his medicine. Sometimes
promises are hard to keep.

PROTEST

Fluffy is **protesting**
because his slice is the smallest...

PULL

Dr. Spotty usually **pulls** teeth. This time he has to
pull the patient from under the chair!
Don't be frightened, Fluffy!

PUMP

"Stop **pumping** ! ! Stop ! ! !" yells Zip.
"I want to drive my car, not fly it !"

PUT

Zip has **put** on Jumbo's boots
to keep his feet dry !

PUNCH

Jumbo was going to **punch** Henry
but Ken stopped him.

PUNISH

Mummy **punished** Rusty
by locking him in the bathroom !

PYJAMAS

One pair of Dad's **pyjamas** fits
both Flip and Flop.

Qq

QUEEN

QUARREL

All of Rhino's ancestors liked to fight and **quarrel**.

QUICKLY

Pinocchio's nose grows **quickly** with every lie he tells.

QUESTION

Before dropping in for a visit, you should always ask the **question** : "Please may I come in ?"

QUEUE

All the Ladybugs are standing in a **queue**. Painty is going to help them look brand new.

QUITE

You have to stay **quite** quiet. You have to stay **quite** still. You have to stand **quite** tall to be the trooper on the hill.

Rr

R r

RAFT

Robinson built a **raft** to take him
away from his desert island.

RAG

Ribbon fell into the river.
Bucktooth is wringing her out like a wet **rag**.

RAGE

Guzzler is in a **rage**
because the editor
says he is ugly. What do you think?

RAIN

When the **rain** stopped,
Frog put away his umbrella,
hopped into the pond
and swam the day away.

RAINBOW

Painty is painting a
rainbow on the wall.
Did he forget any colors?

RAISE

Ozzy has found
a great way to **raise**
some extra money.

RAPIDLY

Rhino went down the stairs just a little too **rapidly**.

RAVENOUS

Guzzler is so **ravenous**,
he's gobbling
the edge of
this page.

REAL

"A **real** snake wouldn't type,"
that's what people say.
But Ribbon is an author snake,
and he types every day.

REEL

Oscar's **reeling** after
being hit on the head
by a flowerpot, again!

REMAIN

You can't **remain** there, Winnie.
You're blocking the harbor.

REMEMBER

Bushytail didn't **remember** to shake the bottle
before taking his medicine.

REMIND

Piglet **reminds** us to wash our ears.
Fluffy **reminds** us to brush our teeth.

It seems that almost everyone
has something to **repair**.
Some are busy doing it,
others don't seem to care.

RESCUE

PC Stop **rescued** Bandit who was trying to escape.

REST

"Where's the **rest** of my worm omelette?" asks Mrs. Hen angrily.

RESTAURANT

Tommy, Timmy, and Scottie have opened the first dog **restaurant**.

RIGHT

Poor Oscar!
It seems that anytime anyone drops anything, he's **right** underneath.

RISE

Bushytail got up early this morning to watch the sun **rise**!

ROCK

Thanks to Winnie, the Captain's boat **rocks** gently on calmer seas.

ROPE

"Zip ought to get a **rope** next time!"
thinks Ribbon.

ROUGH

The waves are very high, the sea is very **rough**.
It might scare most, but Bucktooth's very tough.

RULE

Hotspur certainly
looks as though he
rules the roost in
his new boots!

RUMMAGE

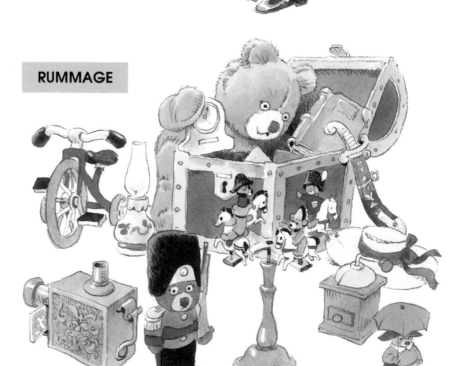

When you **rummage** in an old trunk,
you'll find all sorts of interesting things.

Ss $\mathscr{Ss}$

SAILOR

SAD

Are the Mouse Sisters crying over a **sad** letter or is it the onions?

SAVE

How is Franz going to **save** himself? It is a long, long way down.

SAME

Flip and Flop were both trying to open the door at the **same** time.

SCAMPER

When the commercials come on, Fluffy and his brothers **scamper** away for a snack.

SCARE

Jumping Jack even managed to **scare** Guzzler.

SHIMMER

The dewdrops on the leaves **shimmer** like pearls.

SCOLD

Mrs. Bunnikins **scolds** Dad and Fluffy for playing soccer in the house.

SHINE

Rambler and Robinson like to watch the stars **shining** in the sky.

SHAVE

"Come in," said the barber. "My deal will help you save. You'll only need one cut per year with my super-duper **shave**."

CONTAINER SHIP

OIL TANKER

BARGE

AIRCRAFT CARRIER

FREIGHTER

TUG

CRUISESHIP

HOVERCRAFT

FERRY

FISHING BOAT

TRAINING VESSEL

Will the Captain find a berth
amongst the **ships** in this crowded port ?

SHOCK

Rusty got a big **shock** when he gave Robbie a great big hug.

SHOPLIFTER

Crafty Herbert is hot on the trail of the **shoplifter**.

SHORT

Oscar's ski vacation turned out to be a **short** one.

SIT

Sitting in the tall grass,
resting on a stone,
all his friends have gone away,
and Tip Tap is alone.

SLAM

The minute Joe Crow asked for a loan, Mr. Dollar **slammed** the counter shut.

SLANT

Painty has hung his picture on a **slant** to attract visitors. His plan worked !

SLOPE

Ribbon has found a quick way down the **slope**.

SMELL

Fred **smells** something burning.

SMOOTH

The barber has given Lionstein a **smoother** hairstyle. Do you think he likes it ?

SOFT

The bluebird made a safe landing in Fluffy's **soft** fur.

SPARE

When you go very fast,
you have to take great care.
A scooter only needs two wheels,
but it's best to bring a **spare**.

SPECIAL

Buzz Bee gives her favorite flowers **special** attention and loving showers.

SPECTACLES

"You don't need **spectacles** to see," says Camel. "I can lead you where you need to go."

BASEBALL

TENNIS

BASKETBALL

FOOTBALL

SOCCER

GOLF

POLE VAULT

HIGH JUMP

MOUNTAIN
CLIMBING

SKIING

RUNNING

SAILING

SWIMMING

ROWING

THE CRAWL

BREAST STROKE

BACK STROKE

BOXING

MOTOCROSS

FENCING

CAR RACING

SPRING

Jumping Jack's **spring** is broken.
He's the one that's frightened now!

SQUIGGLE

Painty always signs his pictures
with a **squiggle**.

STAIN

Piglet should know that some foods **stain**
if you don't eat carefully.
He must have gotten carried away.

STEAL

Bandit is annoyed.
Someone **stole** the vase that he **stole** yesterday.

STORM

"What a **storm**," thinks Oscar. "I've never felt
rain drops like this before."

SUSPICIOUS

Bandit has been walking back and forth in front
of the bank all day.
Mr. Dollar is getting **suspicious**.

SWITCH

Joe Crow and Meek Mouse have **switched** hats.
Maybe it wasn't such a good idea.

SWEET

As soft as satin, as clear as the night.
Violet's **sweet** voice is a listener's delight.

SWEETEN

Fluffy **sweetens** his milk
by pouring it into the sugar bowl.

SWOOSH

Winnie **swooshed** to the surface
when she heard Henry singing.

Tt

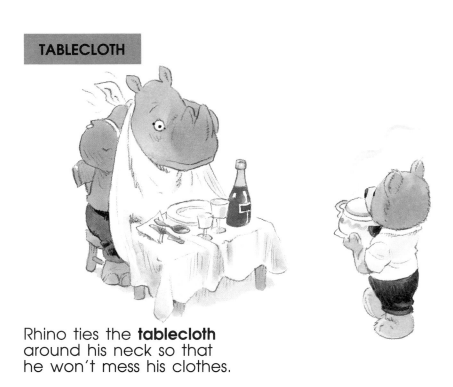

$\mathcal{T}t$

TAILOR

TABLECLOTH

Rhino ties the **tablecloth** around his neck so that he won't mess his clothes.

TAKE

Slowcoach **takes** his house with him wherever he goes.

TAILOR

The **tailor** must have taken the wrong measurements for Attila's new pants.

TALE

Mr. Piggles fell asleep while reading Piglet the fairy **tale** of Sleeping Beauty.

Painty is a **talented** portrait painter, isn't he ?

TASTE

Crock likes the **taste** of snow and he can **taste** a lot at once.

TEAM

Tiger's **team** is sure to win the championship now that Gerry's on the **team**.

TEARS

Henry broke into **tears** when Ken hammered him by mistake.

TEDDY

If you had soft fur and a button nose, do you know what you would be ? Ask **Teddy**, he knows.

TELL

Pardy wants to **tell** the whole world his story. Someone should **tell** Pardy not to litter.

TEMPER

Billy Goat lost his **temper**; this is the third time that Frog has watered him along with the garden !

TEND

Billy Goat reads his poetry longer than he should. His audience **tends** to fall asleep; they think that it's no good.

THAT

Dodger asked Zip the time. Did he do **that** on purpose ?

THEN

If Mrs. Hen takes off these sweaters, **then** she won't be so hot !

THICK

Even the **thickest** fog won't stop Herbert from trying to solve the case.

THIS

Paperette explains that **this** is the only way to get rid of ice cream stains.

THOROUGH

Zip asked Prickles to give his car a **thorough** washing.

THOUGH

Though Wally's caught plenty of fish, he won't have any for supper.

THROW

Teddy **throws** his arms around Dad's neck to thank him for the balloon.

TIGHT

Attila has a feeling his trousers are too **tight**.

TIME

Nothing has gone missing for a long **time** now...
... Dodger's not feeling well.

TIP

Camel feels he needs to give everyone a **tip** in order to be respected.

TOAST

A **toast** can be eaten or just a few words. Beaky **toasts** toucans and all other birds.

TRACE

Teddy loves it when the window gets steamed up. He can **trace** his face on the glass.

TRACK

Bandit fakes Jumbo's **tracks** to trick PC Stop.

TRAFFIC

If Fred wants to drive the fire truck, he needs to learn the **traffic** signs. Can you help him?

TRAP

Tough Cat forgot he had laid a **trap** for Sniffy.

TRAVEL

Mr. Dollar is a snob.
He **travels** in great style.
And when someone stops to say hello,
he doesn't even smile.

TRIAL

If Beaky isn't careful with what he says,
soon he will be on **trial** as well.

TRICK

Lionstein's pupils have played a **trick** on him.

TRIM

Tina used far too many flowers to **trim** her hat.

TRIO

Bim, Bam and Boom form a **trio**.

TROUBLE

The **trouble** with Violet is that
she has a sweet tooth.

TWINS

Flip is like Flop, or Flop is like Flip.
Twins are very much alike.

Uu

UMPIRE

UMBRELLA

Rambler is keeping Robinson's feet dry, and Robinson's **umbrella** is keeping Rambler's head dry. What great friends!

UNABLE

It is too bad that Mrs. Hen is **unable** to keep a secret; Joe Crow is the town gossip.

UNASHAMED

Pinocchio is so **unashamed**, he is telling another one of his lies.

UNBELIEVABLY

Herbert thinks he is **unbelievably** clever. Do you believe it?

UNDER

Fluffy is writing his name **under** a nice valentine he made for Rita Rabbit.

UNDERCARRIAGE

Von Fox must do a quick repair to the **undercarriage** before he can land.

UNEARTH

Mole has **unearthed** an enormous bone. Tommy, Timmy, and Scottie claim it's theirs.

UNEXPECTED

Wally's about to have an **unexpected** swim.

UNHAPPY

Crock is so **unhappy** ! He has a terrible toothache.

UNIQUE

A grasshopper that dances, an elephant that can speak, caterpillars on wheels, these things are **unique**.

UNLIKE

Franz's clothes are **unlike** anyone else's because he lives in the Alps.

UNLUCKY

Unluckily, Painty fell off the roof. Luckily, he didn't hurt himself.

UNPACK

"Sorry Ribbon," says Zip, "but I need to **unpack** the suitcase in the middle."

UNTIDY

Rambler says it's fun to be **untidy**.

UNTIL

Pardy has a letter for Winnie. He'll have to keep patrolling the sea **until** he finds her.

UNUSUAL

Mrs. Piggles decided to give Mr. Piggles an **unusual** gift for Father's Day.

UP

When the window flew open, Jumbo jumped **up** to save Paperette from blowing away.

UPSET

Mrs. Bunnikins is **upset** because nobody remembered her birthday. But she's in for a surprise !

Jumbo's going
upstairs.
Henry's coming
downstairs.

USUALLY

When Mr. Piggles washes the dishes,
usually some of them end up in pieces.

USE

Bucktooth puts his two front teeth to good **use**.

UTMOST

Painty's trying his **utmost** to understand
Chimp's picture.

USELESS

Spinner's taking his web down. He knows
it's **useless** trying to trap Buzz Bee in it.

Vv

VETERINARIAN

VACATION

Ah ! **Vacation** time, again !

VACUUM

Tortoise is showing Mrs. Bunnikins how well his new **vacuum** works.

VANILLA

Vanilla ?
I'm sorry, I thought you asked for sarsaparilla.

VAGUE

Pinocchio hasn't the **vaguest** idea what the answer is. Should he or shouldn't he...?

VEER

No one knows where to go,
which way they should **veer**.
PC Stop is going wild,
his signals are not clear.

VALUABLE

Will Dr. Spotty succeed in extracting Violet's **valuable** necklace that Ozzy has swallowed ?

VEGETARIAN

Sniffy is trying to persuade Tough Cat to become a **vegetarian**.

SPORTS CAR

TAXI

DOUBLE-DECKER BUS

CAMPER

TRUCK

AMBULANCE

RACING CAR

BUS

FIRE ENGINE

WINDSHIELD

TRUNK

LIGHTS

STEERING WHEEL

HOOD

LICENSE PLATE

BUMPER

TIRE

PADDY WAGON

TOW TRUCK

Zip wanted to trade in his car for the latest model. But then he decided his little car was the best **vehicle** for busy traffic.

If Bucktooth wins the canoe race, it will be his
first **victory**. His friends are cheering for him.

Beaky's spouting poetry again !
But Wise Owl is bored stiff by all these **verses**.

Ribbon has stretched as far as she
can to see the **view**.

Tough Cat is **very** hungry.
Sniffy Mouse is **very** frightened.

Brr !
Put on your
woolly **vest**,
Crock, or
you'll freeze
to death !

When you are going to **visit** someone,
it is a good idea to knock before going in.
They might not be expecting you.

VOICE

Wise Owl has nearly lost his **voice** trying to explain the difference between horizontal and vertical lines.

VOLCANO

When a **volcano** erupts, run!!!

VOLTAGE

Robbie's **voltage** is running low. In a minute, he'll be full of energy again.

VOLUNTEER

Teacher asks: "Who would like to **volunteer** to look up a word in the dictionary?"

VOYAGE

Sam and Wally had always wanted to take a **voyage** down south.
Wally is happy but Sam would like to go home.

w W Ww

WOODCUTTER

WAG

Timmy, Tommy and Scottie are trying to see who can **wag** his tail fastest.

WAIT

Robinson is stranded on a desert island. He's **waiting** to be rescued.

WARN

A tug on the thread will **warn** Frog that he's hooked a fish.

WALLPAPER

"Who would want a car made from **wallpaper**?" says Mr. Piggles. Maybe he should ask Scrap and Paperette.

WASHING MACHINE

Poor Sniffy!
He hid inside the **washing machine** to escape from Tough Cat.

WATCH

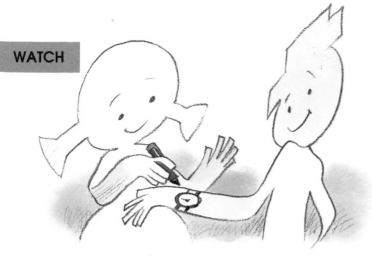

"There !" says Paperette, "now you have a **watch** like everyone else !"

WAVE

Teddy is not too busy swimming to **wave** to his friend, Franz.

WAY

Rhino bent the lamppost on his **way** out of the garage...

... but he straightened it on his **way** back in.

WEAR

Crock is trying on the clothes he used to **wear** when he was a baby. They're a bit small now.

WEIGH

Crafty Herbert is **weighing** a pound of straw and a pound of iron. Which weighs more ?

WELCOME

Robinson got a warm **welcome** when he came home after his travels.

WHALE

Do you know who I am ?
I've got flippers and a tail.
I'm the biggest thing
that swims.
I'm Winnie, I'm a **whale**.

WONDER

Herbert is sitting **wondering**: "When will I solve my first case ?"

WOOD

Pinocchio has found a piece of **wood** and now... he's carving a puppet to play with.

WHO

Flip says the handle is on the right.
Flop says it's on the left. **Who**'s right ?

WORD

Wise Owl is warning Fluffy not to say that **word** again !

WIN

Mr. Piggles' giant carrot **won** first prize at the fair.
It grew so big there was enough for everyone to share.

WORK

WORKER

Tiger is a hard **worker**, but Oscar is lazy!

WORRY

A canoe's the fastest way
to go when you're in a hurry.
But when the water gets this rough,
it's natural to **worry**.

WORST

Joe Crow and Mole **work** for
Mr. Dollar in his gold mine.

Rambler has been told that hitchhiking
is the **worst** thing you can do.
He doesn't listen though, the silly hog.

Poor Tiger !
It wasn't **worth** washing the car.

Fluffy **would** really like to get
into the bathroom... now !

Xx

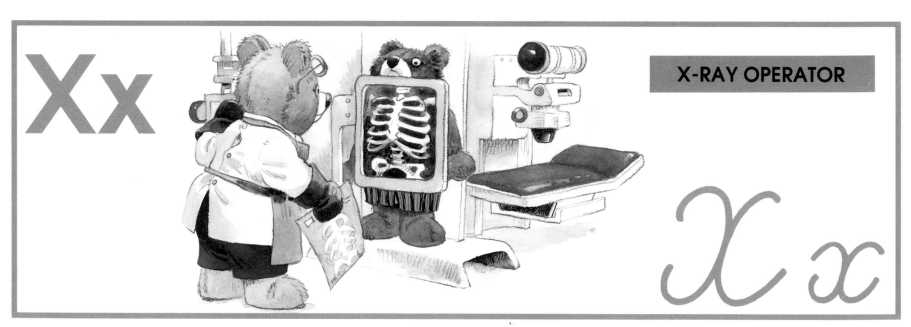

X-RAY OPERATOR

$\mathcal{X}$ x

Wise Owl needs **X-ray** eyes to catch
his pupils copying the answers.

A **xylophone**, when played by one,
goes ting, tang, tong.
A **xylophone**, when played by three,
goes bing, bang, bong.

YACHTSMAN

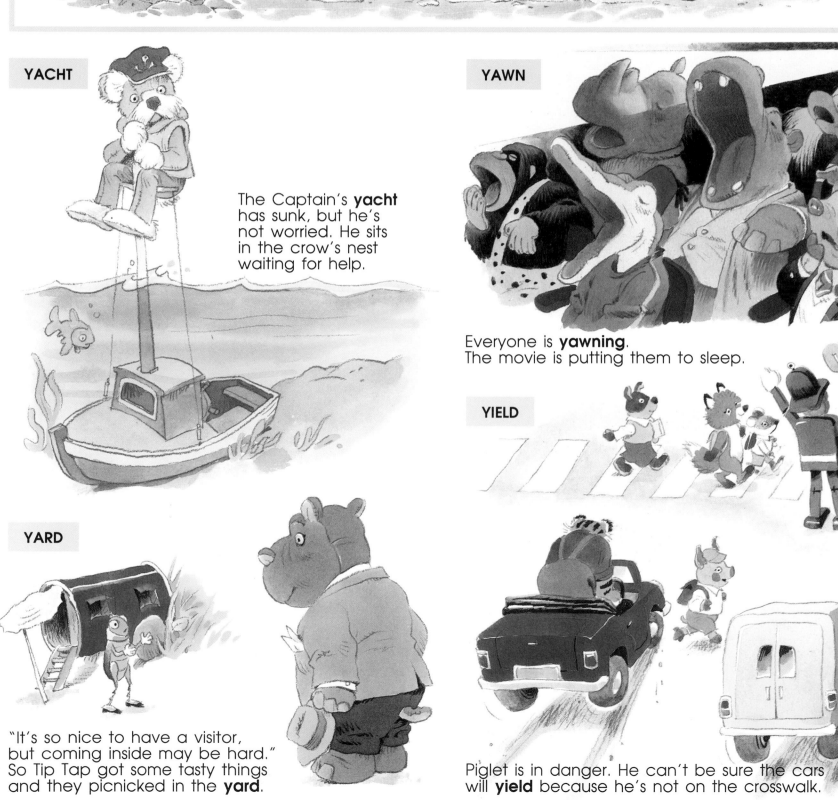

YACHT

The Captain's **yacht** has sunk, but he's not worried. He sits in the crow's nest waiting for help.

YAWN

Everyone is **yawning**. The movie is putting them to sleep.

YIELD

YARD

"It's so nice to have a visitor, but coming inside may be hard." So Tip Tap got some tasty things and they picnicked in the **yard**.

Piglet is in danger. He can't be sure the cars will **yield** because he's not on the crosswalk.

YOGURT

Even though Tip Tap loves **yogurt**, one container can last him for weeks.

YOUNG

This time the **young** bunnies are really up to their necks in hot water !

YONDER

Franz's house is down **yonder** in the valley.

YOUTH

"Oh, sweet **youth**," yearns Joe Crow.
"How was I supposed to know ?
The feathers I was sure would stay
Have now begun to fall away."

Zz

ZOO KEEPER

ZANY

"What a **zany** hairdo you've got !"

ZERO

On a windy day,
Scrap and Paperette's
chances of keeping their feet
on the ground are **zero**.

ZEST

Bluey loves to go real fast,
he loves to take the lead,
he never, ever gets enough.
He has a **zest** for speed.

ZIGZAG

Von Fox is having fun making **zigzags** in the sky.

ZIP

Teddy is a stunt bear ;
he goes by with a **zip**.
If he doesn't watch his speed
he'll have a shorter trip.

ZONE

Jumbo hasn't set up the target quickly enough.
He's in the danger **zone** !

ZOOM

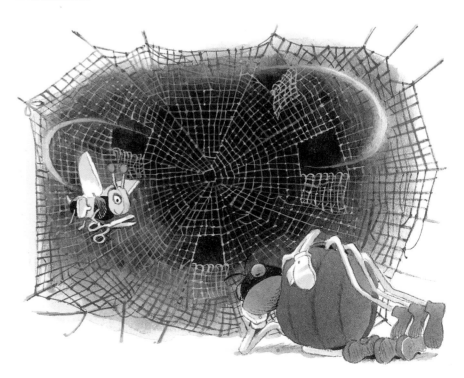

Buzz Bee is **zooming** in
and out of Spinner's web,
making a few windows.